Sonar

KAREN PRICE HOSSELL

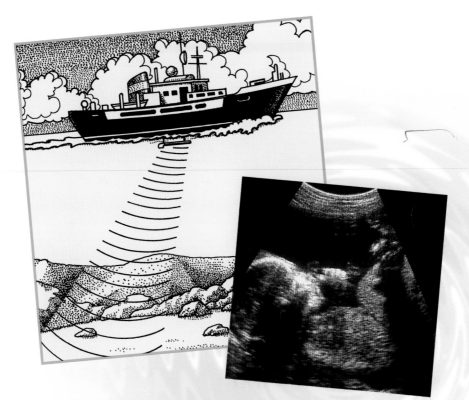

Heinemann Library
Chicago, Illinois

Page layout by Vicki Fischman
Photo research by Amor Montes de Oca
Printed and bound in the United States by Lake Book Manufacturing, Inc.

07 06 05 04
10 9 8 7 6 5 4 3 2

Library of Congress Cataloging-in-Publication Data
Price Hossell, Karen, 1957-
  Sonar / Karen Price Hossell.
    p. cm. -- (Communicating)
Summary: Presents an overview of sound waves and of the history, development, and uses of sonar by both humans and animals.
Includes bibliographical references and index.
  ISBN 1-58810-488-5 (HC), 1-58810-944-5 (Pbk.)
  1. Sonar--Juvenile literature. [1. Sonar.] I. Title. II. Series.
  VK560 .P75 2002
  621.389'5--dc21

                    2002001683

Acknowledgments
The author and publisher are grateful to the following for permission to reproduce copyright material:
Cover photographs (T-B) by Cousteau Society/Getty Images, Tom Pantages p. 4T Adam Hart-Davis/Science Photo Library/Photo Researchers, Inc.; p. 4B Lester Lefkowitz/Corbis; p. 6 Jacksonville Journal Courier/The Image Works; pp. 7, 32 Dorling Kindersley Picture Library; Illustrations pp. 9, 14, 16-17, 24B, 32T, 43T Tom Szumowski/JD Originals; p. 10 Larry Stepanowicz/Visuals Unlimited; p. 11 Fanne White/Photo Researchers, Inc.; p. 12 NOAA; p. 13T Ralph A. Clevenger/Corbis; pp. 13B, 26 Bettmann/Corbis; pp. 15T, 34 USN/Tom Pantages; p. 15B Official Navy Photograph, Naval Undersea Museum, Keyport; pp. 17, 18, 20T, 22, 27, 39B NOAA/Tom Pantages; p. 19L Peter Hvizdak/The Image Works;
p. 19R US Geological Survey/Science Photo Library/Photo Researchers, Inc.; p. 20B Lynette Cook/Science Photo Library/Photo Researchers, Inc.; p. 21B F. S. Westmorland/Photo Researchers, Inc.; p. 21T TSADO/NOAA/Tom Stack & Associates; p. 23 Ralph White/Corbis; p. 24 Academy of Applied Science; p. 25 Scripps Institution of Oceanography/Science Photo Library/Photo Researchers, Inc.; p. 28 Volker Steger/Science Photo Library/Photo Researchers, Inc.; p. 29 Topham/Star Images/The ImageWorks; p. 30 Merlin D. Tuttle/ Photo Researchers, Inc ; p. 31 Jeff Greenburg/Photo Researchers, Inc.; p. 33 Tui de Roy/Minden Pictures; p. 35 Hayne Palmour/North County Times ; p. 36 Carlos Goldin/Science Photo Library/Photo Researchers, Inc.; p. 37 Simon Fraser/Science Photo Library/Photo Researchers, Inc.; p. 38T I. Cartwright/Trip; p. 38B Geoff Tompkinson/Science Photo Library/Photo Researchers, Inc.; p. 39T P. Gontier/Photo Researchers, Inc.; p. 40L Institute of Oceanographic Sciences/NERC/Science Photo Library/Photo Researchers, Inc.; pp. 40R, 41 W. Haxby/Lamont-Doherty Earth Observatory/Science Photo Library/Photo Researchers, Inc.; p. 42T Steve Kaufman/Corbis; 42B Tom Pantages; p. p. 43T Fred J. Maroon/Photo Researchers, Inc.; p. 43C USGS/Tom Pantages; p. 43B Photri, Inc.

Special thanks to Dwight Coleman for his help in the preparation of this book.

About the consultant
Dwight Coleman, director of research at the Institute for Exploration in Mystic, Connecticut, is a marine geophysicist specializing in underwater archaeology and seafloor mapping. He is currently completing a doctorate in Geological Oceanography at the University of Rhode Island and has worked with Dr. Robert Ballard, the explorer who found the *Titanic,* for nearly four years. Coleman has authored or co-authored more than twenty scientific research articles.

Some words are shown in bold, **like this.** You can find out what they mean by looking in the glossary.

Contents

Sound Waves

When you drop a pebble into a pond, you see waves. A circle of pushed-up water forms around the spot where the pebble landed. More and more waves move outward away from the pebble. As the waves spread out, they move less and less water, until finally they stop altogether.

In the same way, when a sound is made, waves form. You cannot see the sound waves, but they are there. They start where the sound starts and move out into the air all around.

The waves made when something drops into a pool of water are often shaped like a circle.

In both of these examples, the waves are a way of moving energy from one place to another. As the energy moves, it makes waves. When you throw a pebble into a pond, the energy goes from you to the pebble to the water. In the water, the energy carried by the waves spreads out farther and farther until it is too weak in any one place to keep moving the water. Energy never actually goes away, though. It just moves from one thing to another.

When you speak, your vocal chords make the air molecules in your throat vibrate. These vibrating molecules make sound waves that travel through the air to another person's ear.

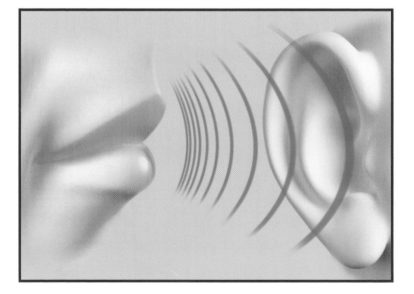

This diagram shows what a sound wave would look like if we could see it.

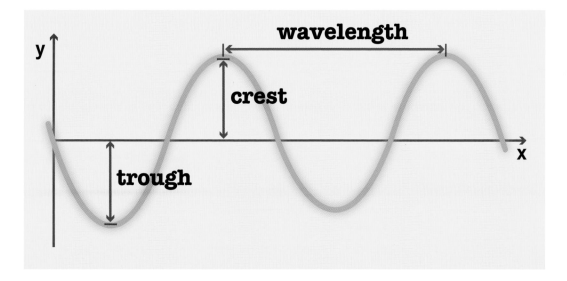

For example, an apple contains energy from the sun, from the soil, and from water. When you eat it, your body uses the energy to keep you alive and to allow you to do things, such as ride a bike and do homework.

Sound waves start with a **vibration.** A person's voice makes sound when the **vocal cords** in the throat vibrate. The moving vocal cords bump into the air **molecules** around them, making the molecules vibrate back and forth, too. These molecules bump into other molecules, and so on. Eventually, the vibrations reach the air molecules near your ears. When these molecules make your eardrums vibrate, you are able to hear the sound.

If you could see sound waves, they would look something like water waves. The highest part of the wave is called the **crest.** The distance between crests is called the **wavelength.** The lowest point of a wave is the **trough.** For water waves, the crest will usually be the same amount above the normal surface as the trough will be below it. This does not work quite the same way for sound waves, but they still move in a similar wave pattern.

Sound Waves and Echoes

Look around you. No matter where you are, there is probably more air around you than there is anything else. The room you are in may have tables and chairs and other people, but most of the room is filled with just air. If a person five feet (1.5 meters) away from you said something right now, the sound waves from his or her voice would probably travel through the air to reach you. If someone was in the next room with the door and windows closed and said something in a normal voice, you probably would not hear it. The sound waves would not have enough energy to pass through the walls. The walls would **absorb** the sound, and it would not pass through. But if that person in the next room screamed or shouted, you might hear it. The loudness and the strength of the voice give the sound waves more energy. If you could see these waves, they would look very "tall." Both the **crests** and the **troughs** would be farther than usual from the normal level. These waves have higher **amplitude.**

Sound waves can also be **reflected.** This happens when sound waves hit a solid object. The waves bounce off the object and are reflected away from it. Imagine you are standing about 30 feet (9 meters) away from the side of a large building. If you shout loudly toward the building, you will hear an echo. The echo is the sound waves coming back to you.

It is usually very easy to hear echoes in places like school gymnasiums.

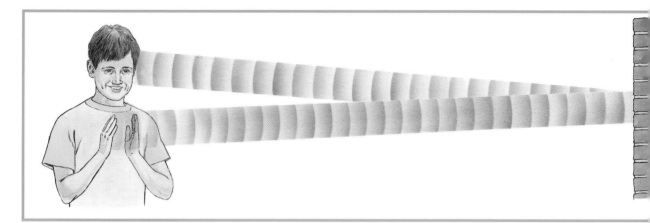

Under the right conditions, a loud sound like a yell or clap will bounce off a wall. The second time you hear the sound, you are actually hearing an echo.

Not all of the waves come back to you, though. The **molecules** in the building will absorb some of the waves. Some of the waves will reflect off the building and go in different directions. If you are closer than 30 feet (9 meters) from an object, the sound of your voice will echo so quickly that you will not be able to tell the difference between the echo and the original sound.

Sound can also travel well underwater. If you have ever gone underwater while you were swimming, you could probably hear the sounds around you. You could hear people talking and dogs barking. They do not sound exactly the same way they do when you are above water, though. Sound moves differently in the water.

Since the early 1900s, people have used underwater sound waves in a special way. They use **sonar** devices to make sounds. When the sounds echo back, they can find out the depth of the ocean or discover objects underwater.

Underwater Sound

Sonar is a shortened form for the words *sound **navigation** and ranging.* That means that sonar can be used to navigate, or find the way around something. It can also be used for ranging, or finding out how far away something is. Sonar is almost always used in water. It has helped scientists and others find out a great deal of information about what is at the bottom of the ocean.

There are three basic kinds of sonar. One kind is called **passive sonar.** This is a one-way type of sonar. A ship with a **receiver** that picks up sounds from another object is said to have passive sonar. The ship receives the sounds, but the ship does not give off sounds. With **active sonar,** a ship or another source not only picks up sounds but also sends out sounds. Active sonar measures how long it takes from the time a signal is sent out to the time the sound waves are **reflected** back to the starting point. This information can be used to figure out how far away the ocean floor or an underwater object is. The third kind of sonar is called an **acoustic communication system.** That means that two ships have the ability to send and receive sonar signals along the same path.

On a ship, the device that makes the sounds is called a **transmitter.** The sound goes from the transmitter through another device called a **transducer.** The transducer changes the transmitter's sound into **vibrations** that are strong enough to travel great distances through water.

A simple use of sonar is finding the depth of a body of water. Sound waves are sent from the ship toward the bottom of the sea. Then the sonar device waits for the echo to reflect off the bottom. This kind of sonar device is often called an **echo sounder.** In the early days of sonar, before computers

Know It

Challenger Deep in the Pacific Ocean is seven miles (eleven kilometers) below sea level. Sound from a ship on the surface travels for almost fifteen seconds before the echo is received.

Active sonar can be used to find the depth of an ocean or lake. It can also be used to locate fish, shipwrecks, or other underwater objects.

kept track of the time, people sending out sonar signals would have to time how long it took the sound to reflect off the bottom of the sea. They knew that in water, sound travels almost 1 mile (1.6 kilometers) per second. If it took two seconds for the echo to return to the receiver, they knew that the sound waves had traveled about 2 miles (3.2 kilometers) in all. But that did not mean that the water was 2 miles deep. The sound waves spent half the time traveling down and half the time traveling back up. That meant people could divide the amount of time in half, or by two, to figure out how long it took the sound to get to the bottom. In this example, the sound waves would have spent one second going down and one second coming back up. Since the sound can travel almost 1 mile through water in one second, the bottom of the water must be about 1 mile below the surface. Using sonar in this way is called **echo ranging.**

Why Can't People Hear Sonar?

An easy way to explain how sound moves is to think of a guitar string. When you pluck the string, it **vibrates** back and forth. These vibrations move the air **molecules** nearby. Sometimes the molecules move closer together. This kind of movement is called a **compression.** When the vibrating molecules move farther apart, this movement is called a **rarefaction.**

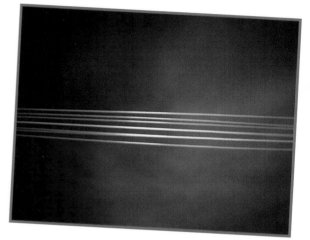

A vibrating guitar string makes the air molecules around it move very fast. The photo was taken using high-speed photography.

Every time an air molecule moves in a compression or rarefaction, it pushes another air molecule that pushes another molecule, and so on. Think of a bunch of marbles lying flat on a table with only tiny spaces between them. When you push one marble, it will move the marbles next to it, and those marbles will move other marbles. In the air, these movements of air molecules are called sound waves.

One property of sound waves is their **frequency.** The frequency is the number of vibrations, or compressions and rarefactions, a sound wave has per second. Each **crest** and **trough** combination on the wave is a **cycle.** The number of these cycles that occur in a second

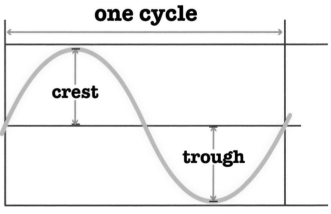

A cycle is completed as a sound wave moves through one trough and one crest.

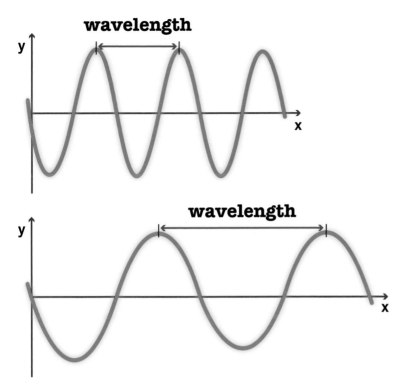

wavelength

y

x

wavelength

y

x

Faster vibrations produce shorter wavelengths, like those shown in the top diagram. The sound wave in the bottom diagram has longer wavelengths. It was produced by a slower vibration.

is called the **hertz.** This unit is named after German scientist Heinrich Hertz. For example, if a sound has 30 cycles in one second, it is measured as 30 hertz, or 30 Hz. Faster vibrations have shorter **wavelengths,** so they have more cycles per second. Slower vibrations have fewer cycles per second.

The human ear can hear sounds that range from about 20 Hz to 20,000 Hz. Anything lower than 20 Hz is called **low frequency.** Another name for a low frequency sound wave is **infrasonic,** meaning "below sound." Sounds above 20,000 Hz are called **high frequency,** or **ultrasonic. Sonar** sends out sounds that are either infrasonic or ultrasonic, so people cannot hear them. Some animals can hear ultrasonic sounds, though.

Dogs can hear sounds that have high frequencies. They can hear many frequencies that humans cannot hear.

11

Early Sonar

Since the early days of **civilization,** people have been trying to find out how deep the rivers and oceans are. Paintings on ancient Egyptian tombs that date from about 1800 B.C.E. show men measuring the depth of the Nile River by putting long poles into the water. The ancient Egyptians also put weights on the ends of long pieces of rope. Then they dropped the weighted end of a rope into the water. They could measure the wet section of rope to see how deep the water was. For thousands of years, this was the best way sailors had of finding the depth of a body of water. They called this system **sounding,** even though at that time they did not measure water depth with sound. Later, sailors used heavy weights that were partly hollow. They were curious about what was on the bottom of the sea. They scraped a weight along the bottom of the sea so they could pick up whatever kind of sand or soil was on the bottom.

In the 1800s, sailors and scientists thought there must be some way to use sound to measure water depth. They tried different ways, but none of them worked very well. In 1914, though, a Canadian scientist and inventor named Reginald Fessenden used a **transceiver** he had developed to locate icebergs in the water. At the time, many people were interested in finding icebergs, including scientists, sailors, and people planning to take ocean voyages.

In 1923, this crew used sounding to find the depth of the ocean around Maui, Hawaii.

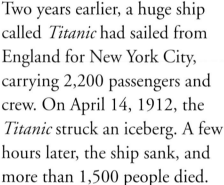

When you see an iceberg from a ship, you really are only seeing a small part of it. Most of an iceberg is underwater. This makes icebergs very dangerous for ships.

Two years earlier, a huge ship called *Titanic* had sailed from England for New York City, carrying 2,200 passengers and crew. On April 14, 1912, the *Titanic* struck an iceberg. A few hours later, the ship sank, and more than 1,500 people died.

This picture of the *Titanic* disaster was made by marine artist Willy Stoewer. Sonar might have prevented many ships from hitting icebergs.

Fessenden and other scientists knew that **sonar** would be the best way to locate icebergs. He sailed on the United States Coast Guard cutter *Miami* with his transceiver, and it used sonar to locate an iceberg that was about 12.5 miles (20 kilometers) away.

Fessenden's invention showed that undersea echoes could be made both up and down and sideways. This was important, because icebergs were often hidden next to ships, not under them. In the 1920s, the Submarine Signal Corporation further developed Fessenden's device and called it the Fathometer™.

Submarines, Sonar, and War

World War I began in Europe in 1914. Germany, Austria-Hungary, Italy, and other countries fought on one side, while Russia, Great Britain, France, and the United States fought on the other side. It was the first war where both **sonar** and submarines were used. Germany had an especially powerful submarine called a U-boat, or undersea boat. One U-boat shot **torpedoes** at a passenger ship called the *Lusitania,* and 1,198 people died. U-boats also sank many ships sending supplies to Great Britain.

Scientists knew that sonar could be used to find enemy ships and submarines. They began to work hard to develop better sonar devices. One French scientist, Paul Langevin, developed better **transducers** that helped sound travel farther through water. With more improvements, sonar operators were able to focus sound waves into beams that acted like sonic searchlights.

How Ships Use Sonar to Find Submarines

Most submarines are painted black so airplanes cannot spot them in the water. Ships can find them, though, by using sonar. Here's how it works: The ship's sonar makes sweeping movements below the ship, and the echoes are timed. When the sonar receives an unusual echo, it might be a submarine. For example, suppose the **receiver** records that the sea bottom is 600 feet (180 meters) below, and that this measurement continues for fifteen minutes. Suddenly, though, the receiver gets an echo that comes from only 200 feet (60 meters) below. The person reading the sonar knows that there are no sudden peaks in the sea bottom, so the object below might be a submarine.

Ships can use very sensitive sonar equipment to find objects like submarines on the seafloor.

14

In 1941, the United States declared war against Japan and entered World War II (fought from 1939 to 1945). Many more submarines were used in World War II than in World War I, as sonar became a valuable tool for navies. Submarines had sonar devices built right into their noses. They often just used **passive sonar,** though, listening for **propeller** and engine sounds from warships and other submarines. They did not send out **pings**—the sounds made by **transmitters**—because they did not want enemy ships to receive the pings and thus be able to help find them.

This is a modern submarine. The sonar operators here are using very advanced equipment.

Sonar and Torpedoes

Torpedoes travel through water and are usually designed to destroy ships and submarines. Many torpedoes use sonar to help locate their targets. One type of torpedo that was used by the United States Navy during World War II was the Mark 24 (MK-24), which had the nickname "Fido." It was launched from aircraft and used passive sonar to find enemy submarines. The torpedo was equipped with several underwater microphones that received sounds from the submarines or

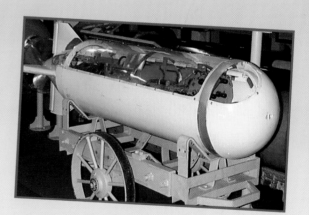

Mark 24 torpedoes used passive sonar to find targets during World War II.

ships. The Mark 24 would then steer in the direction of the sounds. This type of torpedo was responsible for sinking more than 30 submarines during World War II. Today, most torpedoes used by the navy use **active sonar.** They ping the targets and guide themselves in the direction of the echo. Many modern torpedoes can also turn around and reattack their target if they miss the first time.

Kinds of Sonar

The earliest kind of **sonar** made use of **single-beam echo sounders.** These used one beam of sound that could measure the water's depth with one **ping.** This kind of sonar was not always very accurate, because it could take a "picture" of only a small part of the ocean floor.

If ships using this kind of **echo sounding** wanted to "see" more of the bottom of the ocean, they would have to make narrow back-and-forth paths. They could send out beams of sound at many different places in an area. Then they could combine their measurements to get a better idea of what the ocean floor was like there. Scientists and sailors called the ships' back-and-forth movement "mowing the lawn."

In the 1960s, scientists found out how to make **multibeam sonar.** This kind of echo sounding sends out many beams of sound to the ocean floor in many directions. Single-beam sonar could cover only about three feet (one meter) of ocean floor at a time. But multibeam sonar could cover about 300 feet (90 meters) or more.

Single-beam sonar sends down one beam of sound. It shows information about a small part of ocean.

Multibeam sonar can give operators information about a large area of the seafloor.

Sonar devices that are pulled behind a ship often use side-scan sonar. Side-scan sonar sends out wide beams of sound that give information about a large area of the seafloor.

Towfish with side-scan sonar units are pulled behind ships. They are used to study the ocean floor or find schools of fish.

The area of the seafloor reached by multibeam sonar is called a **swath.** Ships using this kind of sonar can collect much more information than they could using single-beam echo sounding, because they can measure more than just one small spot at a time.

Multibeam sonar is sent out from the bottom of a ship and measures the ocean floor below. Another kind of sonar that uses multiple beams of sound is called **side-scan sonar.** This kind of echo sounding is not done directly from a ship. Instead, a device called a **towfish,** or just a "fish," is pulled behind a ship. The fish can send beams of sound in different directions. Some sound waves can go down to the seafloor. Other sound waves go out from the sides of the ship. Side-scan sonar covers a large portion of the undersea area. It is helpful in finding hidden objects that are at the sides of a ship. Some fishers even use sonar like this to help them find large schools of fish to catch!

Mapping the Ocean Floor

For thousands of years, people were not sure what was on the ocean floor. Most people thought it was as flat as the bottom of a small lake or pond. Sailors exploring a new river or other body of water would measure the depth using a weight at the end of a rope. They wanted to make sure that the water was deep enough to sail in safely. With the information they learned from **sounding** the water depth this way, they made maps of the sea bottom. They would mark places that were not deep enough to sail through and places where the sailing was good.

When **sonar** devices were invented, people soon realized they could use them to make detailed maps of the ocean floor. The inventions of **multibeam** and **side-scan sonar** in the second half of the 20th century made mapping easier. Sailors and scientists using this kind of **echo sounding** found they could cover many miles of the ocean floor.

Here is how sonar works to make a map. A special kind of device focuses sound waves so that they become beams. With multibeam and side-scan sonar, many of these beams are made and sent to the seafloor. They cover

This map of the Gulf of Mexico was made using the sounding technique in the late 1800s. The numbers represent the depths of the water in those areas.

GULF OF MEXICO

Soundings on Yucatan Bank from British Admiralty surveys; along Coast of Mexico, within 100 fathoms, from British Admiralty and U. S. Navy surveys; all other soundings from the U. S. Coast Survey

This scientist is looking at a computer display showing information gathered with multibeam sonar. This is part of a U.S. government ocean mapping project.

This map of the ocean near Los Angeles, California was made using a special kind of multibeam sonar. The ocean is blue and green. The land is colored pink.

a large area, so a lot of information can be gathered at one time. When the echoes return to the sonar device, they are changed into electrical energy by a **transducer.** Computers turn the electrical energy into pictures. Some sonar units use personal computers, just like the ones people have in their homes. The pictures are very detailed and show almost every hill and valley in the **seabed.** They can show even small pebbles and stones. The sonar equipment saves the pictures on a computer in strips that correspond to the path of the ship. The strips are put together like a puzzle to make a **mosaic.** The mosaic is then put onto a large map that serves as a reference.

Two-thirds of Earth is covered by oceans. It will take a long time to make complete maps of the bottoms of all of the oceans. However, scientists and engineers are able to make the job a little easier with sonar that is more advanced and uses the latest developments in **technology.**

Finding Faults

Undersea mapping using **sonar** is very useful to sailors, but it can help other people, too. One thing the sonar maps are good for is helping to locate **faults.** These are breaks in Earth's surface, or **crust.** In places where the crust is broken, the land on each side of the fault will sometimes move. This shifting of the parts of Earth's surface causes earthquakes.

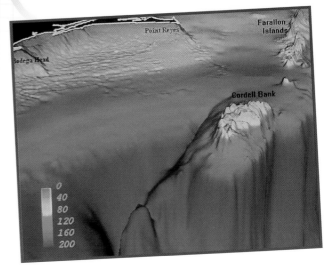

This is a sonar map of the Farallon Islands near San Francisco. The blue area shows where the ocean floor drops off and the water becomes very deep.

Until recently, scientists knew for sure only about faults that were on land. They were aware that there must be faults under bodies of water, but they could not be sure where these breaks were. When sonar ocean mapping began, it helped to show the locations of undersea faults. This knowledge will help scientists who study earthquakes understand how the faults move. They will also be able to better predict when and where an earthquake may occur. Other disasters can also happen

An 1883 tsunami in Indonesia might have looked like this as it approached a nearby island.

when faults move underwater. The movement can cause a **tsunami,** a giant wave that is also called a **tidal wave.** The sonar maps can help scientists find out if anything like this is going to happen, too.

Faults are not just on land and in the ocean. For example, scientists know for sure that there is a fault in the bottom of Lake Tahoe, Nevada. This fault was found during a sonar **scan** of the lake.

Science Underwater

When sonar mapping locates something that looks like it may be a fault, **marine geologists** sometimes use **submersibles** to check it out. The submersibles are small vehicles that go deep into the sea. Some submersibles carry people. Others go down so far that people would not be safe inside them. Instead, the submersibles carry cameras that take pictures of the faults. These kinds of submersibles are operated by **remote control.**

These submersibles can dive deep down into the ocean. Without submersibles like these, scientists could not explore and do research at the bottom of the ocean.

Underwater Archaeology

In the deep sea, where there is little natural light, visibility is low. **Sonar** allows us to "see in the dark" because sound travels much better than light underwater. As a **towfish** with **side-scan sonar** sweeps over the bottom of the sea, sound waves transmit over fixed distances. Objects that are lying on the bottom—even objects that are partially buried—can bounce sound waves back to the towfish. The stronger the **reflection,** the more the object stands out on the sonar image.

For this reason, side-scan sonar is a popular tool for locating shipwrecks and other underwater **archaeological** sites. Many of the sonar images that are produced look exactly like shipwrecks, but occasionally they do not—especially if the shipwreck is very old, buried, or damaged.

Sonar is also used to make detailed maps of the sites. These maps are useful to an archaeologist for measuring distances between and sizes of distinct features of the site. Just like **marine geologists** study the seafloor and map **faults,** a marine archaeologist studies underwater sites of human history.

This is a sonar image of the *Monitor,* a famous ship that sank in 1862 off the eastern coast of the United States. The *Monitor* was a Union ship that had been used in many battles against the Confederates during the Civil War.

Together with other techniques, sonar has been used to locate and gather information on historically important shipwrecks such as the *Monitor* and *Titanic*. Sonar has also been used to locate shipwrecks that are thousands of years old. Some ancient shipwrecks found in the Mediterranean Sea contained ceramic jars that carried wine and other items for trade. Sonar has also been used to search for **prehistoric** archaeological sites.

This sonar image shows the wreck of the *Titanic*. The *Titanic* sank on its first trip across the Atlantic Ocean in 1912.

Looking for a Monster

In October 1987, 24 boats gathered on a lake in northern Scotland. The boats turned on their **echo sounders** and began to move slowly across the lake. They were not mapping the lake's bottom or looking for shipwrecks. They were searching for a monster.

The lake was Loch Ness. Many people think that this loch—the Scottish word for *lake*—is the home of a large, mysterious sea creature. The creature is often called the Loch Ness Monster, or Nessie. In 1987, a group from a company that makes **sonar** units gathered the boats and began the search, called Operation Deepscan. Because the boats kept moving as they used sonar, other boats followed them to check on anything unusual they reported.

The boats went up and down the 23-mile-long (37-kilometer-long) lake. Several unusual things were found on sonar. But when the other boats used sonar to check the odd findings, they found nothing.

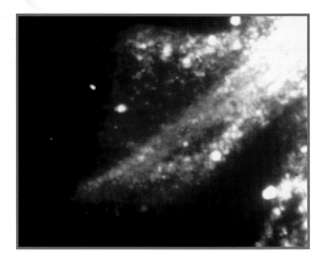

This photograph was taken in 1975 with the aid of **side-scan sonar.** Some people say it shows the flipper of the Loch Ness monster.

This is the popular image of the Loch Ness monster that many people have today. It is similar to the way scientists describe a type of ancient dinosaur.

It was not the first time people had tried to find the monster with sonar. As early as the 1950s, people made sonar searches of the lake. Usually, though, they searched with just one boat. One man using sonar found what he thinks is a large **cavern** in the lake. Some people think the monster may hide in the cavern most of the time. In 1997, something large and moving was found using sonar.

Despite all the searching, there is still no conclusive scientific evidence of the existence of the Loch Ness Monster. Nevertheless, the legend and mystery surrounding the loch continues. And since people love to solve mysteries, they will keep looking for a monster in the waters of Loch Ness.

Finding Fish

Many people who like to fish and who own boats use sonar to locate fish. The sonar **scans** the water under and next to the boat. Fish show up as blurs on a screen inside the boat. People who do ice fishing use sonar, too. They use hot water to make a hole in the ice, then put a **transmitter** into the water. Fish-finding sonar cannot tell what kind of fish is in the water, though, or how big the fish is. It can only recognize that something is moving in the water.

Above is an image of a goldfish and a ping-pong ball on "Fish-TV," an advanced three-dimensional sonar system.

Sonobuoys

Many navies use special airplanes called antisubmarine patrol craft to fly over the ocean, looking for submarines. The people in the airplanes have a hard time finding submarines with the naked eye, though. The ocean is so deep in most places that it is impossible to see very far down into it. The waves also make it harder to see anything underwater very clearly. In addition, submarines are often painted black so they can hide better, and many modern submarines are quiet and hard to find.

For these reasons, the airplane crews have to do more than simply look down into the ocean for submarines. Instead, the airplanes drop **sonobuoys** into the water. The sonobuoys float at the water's surface. Part of each buoy is above the water, and part of it is beneath the water. The part that is under the water contains a **sonar** device. It sends out signals to find whatever might be in the sea below. A radio is attached to the part of the buoy above the water. The echoes that the sonar unit receives are sent to the radio. Then the radio sends the information to the airplane.

Military aircraft like this S-3A Viking can carry sonobuoys or sonar-activated **torpedoes** and **mines.** The S-3A Viking can be used to hunt enemy submarines.

Sometimes, the military uses a helicopter instead of an airplane to drop sonobuoys. The buoys hang from a long cable attached to the helicopter. The helicopter dips the buoys into the water and waits for signals. A helicopter can actually fly along with a sonobuoy attached while the buoy sends out its sonar signals.

Scientists also use sonobuoys to listen for whales and to track fish. They attach sonar units to the fish. As the fish swim, their sonar units send out signals. Scientists listen for the signals and learn about where fish swim. They even attach sonar onto lobsters so they can track the lobsters with sonobuoys. As scientists learn more about the behavior of different sea creatures, they can better understand how to make sure the animals are kept safe and healthy.

Helicopters are often used to drop sonobuoys into the ocean.

Underwater Volcanoes

On the Big Island of Hawaii, volcanic eruptions are very common. Twenty miles (32 kilometers) to the southeast, a new Hawaiian island will form when Loihi Seamount, an active underwater volcano, erupts and grows to form an island. Volcanic eruptions occur frequently on the seamount, and scientists are interested in understanding the growth of islands. With help from the United States Navy, scientists from the University of Hawaii have used sonobuoys to try to locate the exact position of the underwater eruptions. The scientists had been monitoring the seamount when a series of earthquakes occurred, indicating the underwater volcano was about to erupt. Navy airplanes dropped a number of sonobuoys to record the sounds from the undersea eruption. This exercise helped the navy as well as the scientists because they were able to practice dropping sonobuoys accurately. This is very important for antisubmarine warfare.

Sonar and Robots

Although **sonar** is mainly used for underwater study and exploration, it can also work in other ways. One way sonar is used outside of the water is in robots. Inventors make robots that can do many things. The robots can clean floors, do errands for people who cannot walk easily, and guide wheelchairs. The robots cannot really see, but many of them get around just fine—using sonar.

Know It

An engineer at Yale University made a robot that uses sonar the same way bats and dolphins do. Sound waves come from its "mouth," and it has "ears" to receive the echoes.

Robots can have built-in **sensors** that use sound and echoes to guide them from place to place. For example, when a robot gets too close to a wall, it can tell where it is from the echoes its sensors receive. It can stop safely before it hits the wall. Some robots have many sonar units in a ring all around them. These units send out and receive signals in all directions. That way, the robots will not run into anything in front of them, behind them, or next to them.

One kind of robot cleans floors by traveling in paths along the floor. It does not bump into objects because it has sonar sensors that let it know when something is in the way. Another kind of robot floor cleaner is a vacuum cleaner. It uses

Sonar ranging sensors can be connected to toy robots like this one.

sonar that sends signals to a "brain" that tells it where to go. The vacuum stops when it senses an object in its way. Then it turns and goes in another direction.

Many people make robots just for fun. Robots like these will often have sonar sensors. People even enter contests to see whose robot will work the best to do certain tasks or to respond to certain commands. The more people work with robots and sonar sensors, the better robots they are able to build. Who knows—maybe someday robots will do all of your housework!

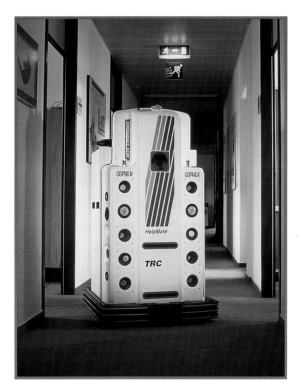

Domestic robots can work in many places. This robot uses ultrasonic sensors to find its way around a hospital.

How Does It Work?

Sonar sensors on robots use some very complicated **technology**. A small **transmitter** on the robot sends out **ultrasonic** signals that bounce off walls and objects. The echoes are received by a small **transducer** on the robot. These components can also be placed on a moving platform to allow the sonar to **scan** in different directions. A sonar instrument is integrated with the other electronics that control the robot. The ultrasonic signals are used to compute distances to the objects. The computer in the robot can then determine how it needs to travel to reach or avoid the object. Similar ultrasonic sonar devices can be mounted on the manipulator, or the robot's "hand," to help it grab objects. Some advanced robots can use very precise sonar to "look" for objects. In addition to the precision electronics that are needed to control the sonar, some very complicated computer processing is needed to use the sonar data. The more accurate a robot's sonar and computer systems, the "smarter" it can be.

Bats and Sonar

Have you ever wondered how bats can fly around at night without bumping into things? There are more than 900 different kinds of bats, and some can see well enough to **navigate** in the darkness. More than half of bats, though, use **sonar** to tell where they are going. This ability is called **echolocation,** because the bats use echoes to locate, or find, objects.

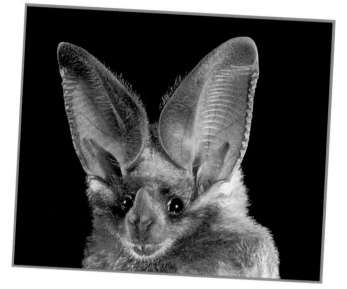

Many bats have very large ears that help them hear echoes. This is a California leaf-nosed bat.

The kinds of bats that use echolocation have big ears. Their ears act as **receivers** to pick up even small sounds, and especially one certain kind of sound. These bats make squeaking sounds with such **high frequencies** that the human ear cannot hear most of them. Most of the sounds come from a bat's voice box, but some bats make sounds with their nostrils. As the bats fly, they make these **ultrasonic** squeaks the whole time. The sounds bounce off objects in their path, and the echoes return to the bats' ears.

These echoes help the bats in two main ways. First, the bats are able to fly safely by using the information they get from echoes. They pay attention to how long it takes for the echoes to come back. This helps them figure out how far away things are, so they do not run into objects as they fly. Second, the echoes help the bats find food. Bats eat insects, and they can locate even the tiniest insects, such as mosquitoes, by listening for their **reflected** sounds to bounce back. Both the ability to travel safely and the ability to find food are very important for the bats. They would not be able to survive without echolocation.

Scientists at Brown University in Rhode Island have been studying brown bats, a type that is common in the United States. They discovered that brown bats can hear two different echoes if the sound they make bounces off two separate objects. The scientists also believe that the bats can tell what kind of object is in their way just by using echolocation. Some bats seem to be able to tell what kind of moth is a few feet away from them just from the kind of echoes that reflect from the moth. Scientists would like to learn how the bats can figure out things like these. They hope to use that knowledge to develop better sonar for the United States Navy.

Can Humans Use Echolocation?

Some scientists have done research to see if humans are able to echolocate the way bats and dolphins do. They blindfolded people and asked them to make noises to see if they could locate objects. Many people found out they could locate objects this way. However, they were not nearly as good at it as some animals! Other scientists have studied blind people. Many people discover that when they lose their sight, their sense of hearing improves. Some scientists believe that blind people use a form of echolocation to get around.

What do you think? You could try it by closing your eyes and making noise to see if you can get around your bedroom. Pick up everything off the floor first, though. And walk slowly so that you do not bump into something hard if your echolocation skills are not very good.

Studies have found that some blind people have increased hearing abilities.

Dolphins, Whales, and Sonar

Animals called toothed whales use **echolocation,** too. They make clicking and whistling sounds, called **trains,** and use the echoes to find their way around and to locate food. Toothed whales include dolphins and porpoises, as well as whales like sperm whales, beaked whales, beluga whales, and narwhals.

The clicking sounds dolphins and porpoises make come out of their bodies through an organ called a **melon.** The melon is made up of fat and is at the top of a dolphin's head, just in front of its **blowhole.** The sounds travel forward in a kind of beam of sound. The echoes return to the dolphin near the jawbone, then take their messages to the dolphin's brain.

Studies done by marine biologists have shown that dolphins seem to use their **sonar** not just to locate food, but also to damage the hearing of the fish they hunt. Scientists have recorded dolphins making banging and buzzing sounds

melon

Toothed whales use sounds not only for echolocation, but also for communication with other members of their species.

Dolphins and many other toothed whales use echolocation to find both food and predators.

with their sonar when they are chasing fish. The sonar bothered the fish so much that they ended up swimming in circles or dying.

Whales make clicks or whistles in their **nasal sac systems.** This system is made of air-filled pouches that are just behind the whale's melon. The sounds go through the melon and out in front of the whale. The whale can locate objects by listening for the echoes. The echoes are received in an area near the whale's lower jawbone. They travel from the jawbone into the brain.

Using echolocation, dolphins, porpoises, and whales can tell not only the size and shape of an object, but also how far away it is and how fast it is moving. They also make clicking and whistling sounds when they want to communicate with each other.

Most scientists think that only toothed whales use echolocation. Scientists also think that whales beach themselves—come up onto the beach instead of staying out in the ocean—when something happens to harm their sonar systems. The whales cannot **navigate** without sonar, so they keep swimming until they reach the beach.

Sick Whales

Some researchers believe that human sonar use can cause marine mammals such as whales and dolphins to strand themselves on beaches. Human sonar use is thought to produce increased noise in the ocean that causes damage to mammals' ears. This disturbs their ability to navigate. Other researchers do not believe that human sonar use causes marine mammal stranding, as there is no direct evidence. It has been shown, however, that whales will not stay in areas where **low frequency** sonar is in use.

These volunteers are trying to save 65 pilot whales that beached themselves in New Zealand.

Finding Mines

During wartime, the navies of the countries that are fighting often plant **mines** in the ground and in the sea. Some mines are placed on the **seabed**. Others are held to the seabed by an anchor. They float a few feet above the seabed to be closer to ships. The mines are small bombs that are set to explode if something triggers them. The sound of a ship's engine, for example, can make them explode. Some mines can be set so that several boats can pass by unharmed. Then another boat sails by and the mine explodes, destroying the ship and killing people.

For years **sonar** has been used to find mines. A sonar device can make a printout of an area where mines are located. Ship captains can then use the printout as a map and **navigate** around the mines.

Modern mines are designed so that they are hard for sonar to **detect.** But the United States Navy has found a way to locate most mines. Since 1960, the navy has been training dolphins to find mines using their built-in sonar—their ability to **echolocate.** The dolphins are in no danger, because they are too light to set off the mines. The dolphins attach a special **buoy** to each mine they find. Ships passing by see the buoys and know to avoid the area.

The navy has trained more than 60 dolphins to protect its ships and find mines.

Dolphins like this one are trained by the navy to locate mines and perform other important tasks underwater.

The dolphin program is called the Marine Mammal Program. Sea lions and one whale have also been trained to help the navy. The mammals are trained to do other jobs as well. Some of them carry tools from one ship to another or between ships and people working in the water.

Some of the dolphins were used in the Persian Gulf War. This fighting took place in 1991, with the United States and other countries on one side against Iraq. The United States Navy trained six dolphins to protect the ship *LaSalle* by using their sonar. The dolphins looked for enemy swimmers trying to plant mines on or near the ship. The dolphins could detect the swimmers using echolocation. Then they warned a lookout person on the nearest warship. These dolphins also found mines planted in the Gulf.

Know It

In addition to helping the United States Navy, dolphins can help search-and-rescue teams locate victims of boating accidents or cars that have fallen off bridges.

When they complete a task correctly, dolphins are rewarded with a treat of fish.

Ultrasound

Sonar uses sounds that have **frequencies** that are too low or too high to be heard by the human ear. Sounds that are too high are called **ultrasound.** Ultrasound is also the name of a machine used in doctors' offices. The machines use sound waves to see inside the human body. The waves **reflect** off organs inside the body and help create a picture of what the organs look like. The machines have to use sounds with **wavelengths** even smaller than the organs and bones they are trying to "see." Sounds with these small wavelengths have a very **high frequency**—that is why this type of sonar is called ultrasound.

People who know how to use ultrasound to look inside the body are called **sonographers.** They press a small device on a person's skin near the organs they want to check. If they want to see the person's heart, for example, they put the device near the heart. One of the most frequent uses for ultrasound is to see a **fetus** inside its mother. The sonographer rubs the small device over the mother's abdomen. The sound waves go into the mother's body and send back echoes. A computer turns the echoes into a picture, called a **sonogram.** The device is usually hooked up to a computer monitor, so the sonographer and patient can both see the picture.

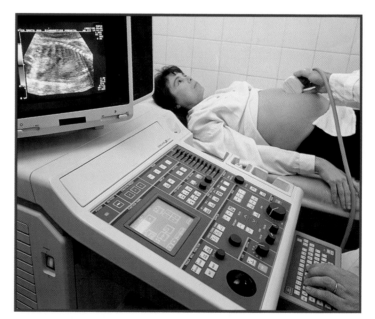

A doctor is using ultrasound to examine this pregnant woman. The red area on the video screen shows blood flowing in the fetus' heart.

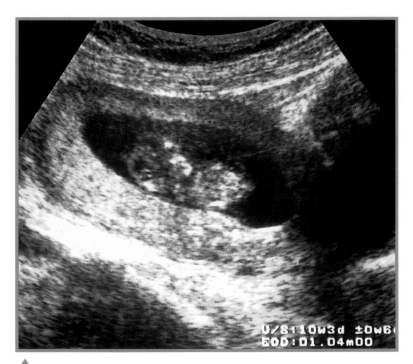

This is an ultrasound **scan** of a nine-week-old fetus inside its mother. The fetus is almost two inches (five centimeters) long at this stage. Ultrasound can show if a fetus is growing normally.

Another way ultrasound **imaging** can be used is to look for problems inside the body. Doctors may use this kind of test to try to figure out why someone is in pain. They may use the device to look for a **tumor** growing inside the body. If everything is normal, the sonogram will show pictures of healthy organs. But if anything strange or unusual appears on the sonogram, a doctor may decide to investigate more. He or she may order more tests. The sonogram's information can even help doctors decide if they should perform surgery on a patient.

Careers in Sonar

A person who is interested in **sonar** can find many ways to use that interest. Sonar **technology** is improving all the time. People are needed, though, to continue researching and improving the technology.

The navy is a good place to learn about how to use sonar. Many sonar operators, however, work on submarines. Do you mind being in small spaces for long periods of time? If so, a submarine may not be a good place for you to work. People who work on submarines often have to live on them underwater for weeks, or even months, at a time.

Robotics is another area where sonar skills can be used. This is an exciting field that has many possibilities. If you like making things or figuring out new ways to do things, you may want to look into a career in robotics. In marine robotics, people work on robots that do all kinds of things underwater. Most people who like doing this kind of work are good at math and science.

Archaeologist

Underwater archaeologists use sonar to locate shipwrecks and other underwater evidence of human cultures.

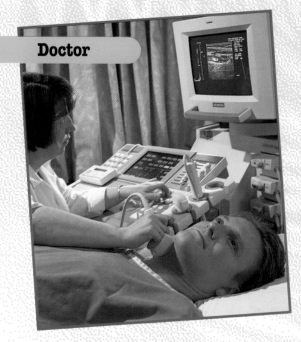

Doctor

Ultrasound is used by doctors to examine a number of areas inside the body.

Acoustic Engineer

Among other things, acoustic engineers study the noise created by industrial machines and motors.

People who are interested in working with computers can use their skills to design **software** to use for sonar mapping and other sonar technology. People who prefer working with **hardware** could use their skills to design machines that **transmit** and receive sonar signals.

Acoustic engineers work with all kinds of sounds, not just sonar. They could work with musicians, architects, film directors, or other people who are interested in how sound is recorded or controlled.

Sonographers use **ultrasound** devices to take "pictures" of what is going on inside the human body. If you are interested in the medical field, you may want to look into this career.

Other careers that are related to sonar include dolphin trainer, underwater **archaeologist,** and **marine engineer.** All of these careers involve hard work, but they are rewarding as well.

Scientist

Phantom robots are used by scientists at the National Oceanic and Atmospheric Administration. Together with sonar, the robots help find objects underwater.

Appendix A: Ocean Maps

Sonar is the most common tool used today for mapping the ocean floor. **Multibeam sonar** gives very detailed depth information by mapping a strip of the ocean floor beneath the track of the ship. Multiple parallel **swaths** are merged together to produce large, detailed depth maps of the bottom. **Side-scan sonar** does not give detailed depth information, but it "paints a picture" of the seafloor. This is because individual objects and other small geologic features can be **detected** by

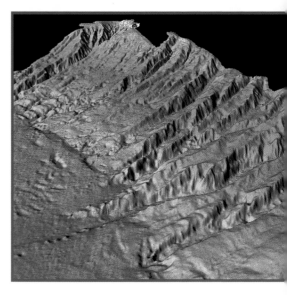

These deep underwater canyons are off the coast of New Jersey. The canyons were cut by underwater avalanches of mud and sand. The colors in this image indicate depth: white is near sea level, while green indicates a depth of 8,200 feet (2,500 meters).

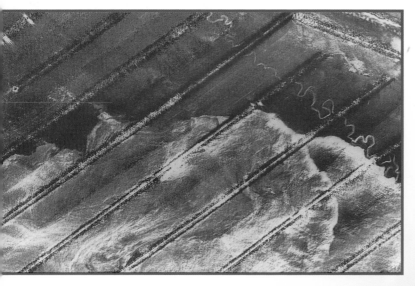

This image of the seafloor in the Gulf of Mexico is a **mosaic.** The diagonal lines are the track of the ship towing the side-scan sonar. The lines are about twelve miles (twenty kilometers) apart. There is a long channel in the upper right part of the image.

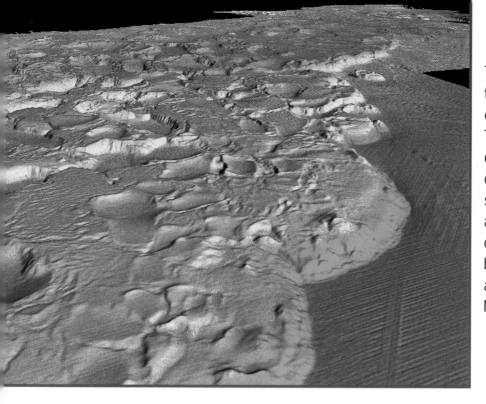

The **seabed** near the coast of Louisiana drops off very quickly. The high area in orange and yellow is called the continental shelf. The rough appearance of the continental shelf has been created by mud and sand from the Mississippi River.

side-scan sonar that multibeam sonar cannot show. The information from multibeam sonar can be combined with the images from the side-scan sonar to give very detailed, accurate ocean maps. Multibeam sonar depth information can be viewed in three dimensions. This lets **marine geologists** map and interpret formations on the seafloor.

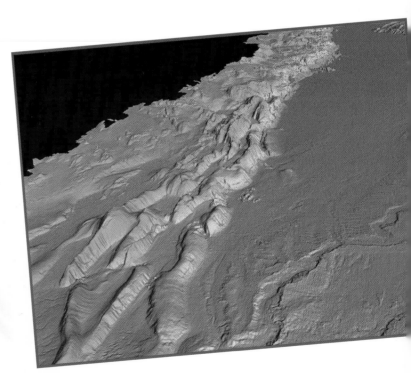

The seafloor near Oregon has long ridges. Like many mountain ranges, these ridges are formed when one plate of Earth's **crust** is pushed under another.

Appendix B: Sonar Tools

A lot of equipment is needed to operate underwater **sonar** systems. The kind of equipment that is used depends on what is being looked for and where. For example, the United States Navy, which is interested in finding enemy submarines, uses sonar differently than scientists who study the ocean floor. Sonar **transmitters** and **receivers** are usually mounted on a ship, submarine, or **towfish.** Sonar tools are built differently to transmit and receive certain **frequencies** and to operate at certain depths. Today, sounds and data are recorded using computer equipment. The computers have programs that can process, play back, and print sonar data. This helps sonar operators analyze and interpret the data. In the early days of sonar **technology,** data was often plotted on paper.

This is the sonar room on the United States Navy submarine USS *Omaha.* Sonar is used for submarine **navigation** and **torpedo** firing.

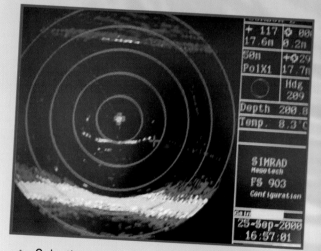

Scientists look at sonar displays like this one to study the ocean floor.

These sonar operators are working on a United States Navy submarine.

Towfish have **side-scan sonar** that collects information on a wide area of the ocean floor. Towfish can also **scan** for schools of fish.

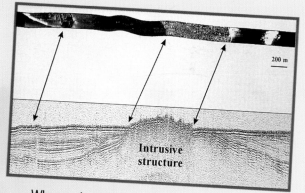

200 m

Intrusive structure

When scientists take samples of the ocean floor, they use sonar printouts like this one to find the best place for the sample.

This sonar equipment is being lowered off the rear deck of a United States Navy ship.

43

Glossary

absorb   take in

acoustic communication system
system that uses sound waves and
beams to communicate

acoustic engineer   person who studies
the control, production, effects,
reception, and transmission of sound

active sonar   sonar system that can
both transmit and receive signals

amplitude   measurement of the
height of a sound wave; the distance
from the zero point to a crest
or trough

archaeology   study of how people
lived in the past. An archaeologist is
a person who studies how people
lived in the past.

blowhole   hole in the top of the head
of whales, dolphins, and porpoises

buoy   floating object placed in the
sea as a marker

cavern   large cave

civilization   way of life specific to a
particular time and place

compression   air movement
caused by the first move of a
vibrating object

crest   highest point of a sound wave

crust   top part or surface of a planet

cycle   in sound, the combination
of the crest and the trough of a
sound wave

detect   find or locate

echo ranging   finding the depth of
a body of water by timing echoes
that return from sound waves sent
by sonar

echo sounder   device that sends
sound to the bottom of the sea

echolocate   find an object using
reflected sound. Some animals make
sounds and listen for the echoes to
return to them.

fault   break in the earth's crust

fetus   unborn baby

frequency   number of vibrations a
sound wave makes per second

hardware   mechanical parts used to
make something

hertz   unit for the number of
sound wave cycles per second;
abbreviated Hz

high frequency   sound that measures
more than 20,000 hertz, or Hz

imaging   action of producing a visual
picture of something

infrasonic   low-frequency sound waves that cannot be heard by humans

low frequency   sound that measures less than 20 hertz, or Hz; people cannot hear low-frequency sounds

marine engineer   person who designs and helps produce boats, submarines, and underwater structures

marine geology   study of the ocean floor, including the mapping of underwater faults

melon   round organ in the forehead area of some whales and most dolphins and porpoises

mine   explosive device planted underground or underwater

molecule   tiny particles that make up an object or substance. Molecules are invisible to the naked eye but are part of everything.

mosaic   map made up of strips of sonar data that are put together to make a large map

multibeam sonar   type of sonar device that makes many beams of sound and sends them into the sea

nasal sac system   part of a whale that produces whistles or clicks; located near the top of the whale's head

navigate   find one's way around; get around without running into objects

passive sonar   sonar device used to listen for other ships

ping   sound made by a transmitter sending out sonar sound waves

prehistoric   before people started writing down or recording things

propeller   device with blades attached to a center. The blades turn and move a vehicle, such as a ship or an airplane.

rarefaction   air movement caused when a vibrating object returns to its starting position or continues to move beyond that position

receiver   device that takes in signals from another source. In sonar, a receiver picks up echoes from the pings sent out by a transducer or transmitter.

reflect   bounce off. Echoes are sound waves that have reflected off a solid object.

remote control   operating something from a distance

robotics   everything that deals with robots, including their design, construction, and operation

scan   in sonar, examination of an area with sonar equipment

seabed   bottom or floor of the sea or ocean

sensor   device that detects something. A sonar sensor sends out sound waves and receives echoes

side-scan sonar   sonar device that sends beams of sound out sideways using a towfish

single-beam echo sounder   sonar device that uses one beam of sound sent straight under the ship or boat

software   program that makes a computer work

sonar   system that locates objects using echoes from sound waves it sends out. The word stands for *sound navigation and ranging.*

sonobuoy   floating object placed in the water to receive or send out sonar signals. It also transmits them by radio back to a station.

sonographer   person with training to use ultrasound

sonogram   image of a part of the body made using ultrasound

sounding   finding out the depth of a body of water

submersible   small watercraft used for undersea research

swath   wide path

technology   special knowledge and materials used in a particular area or career

tidal wave   giant sea wave often caused by an earthquake or underwater volcano

torpedo   underwater weapon used to destroy ships or submarines. Some torpedoes have sonar devices.

towfish   sonar device pulled behind a ship; the towfish is attached to the ship by a cable. Towfish are used for side-scan sonar and send out many beams of sound.

train   series of clicks or whistles a whale, porpoise, or dolphin makes when it is echolocating

transceiver   something that acts as both a receiver and a transmitter

transducer   in sonar, device that changes sound into electricity or electricity into sound

transmitter   in sonar, device that sends out sound waves or signals

trough   lowest point of a sound wave

tsunami   giant sea wave caused by an earthquake or by an underwater volcano

tumor growth on or inside the body

ultrasound high-frequency sound that cannot be heard by humans. Ultrasonic frequencies are used to make an image of the inside of the human body.

vibration action of something being moved back and forth

vocal cord cord in the throat that vibrates to make sound

wavelength distance between crests of a sound wave

More Books to Read

Ackerman, Diane. *Bats: Shadows in the Night.* New York: Crown Publishers, 1997.

Cobb, Vicki. *Bangs and Twangs: Science Fun with Sound.* Brookfield, Conn.: The Millbrook Press, 2000.

Fredericks, Anthony D. *Exploring the Oceans: Science Activities for Kids.* Golden, Colo.: Fulcrum Publishing, 1998.

Searle, Bobbi. *Inventor's Handbook: Robots.* San Diego: Silver Dolphin, 2000.

Index